GLOBAL WARMING

THE THREAT OF EARTH'S CHANGING CLIMATE

LAURENCE PRINGLE

SeaStar Books · NEW YORK

The author thanks Dr. R. A. Houghton, Senior Scientist at The Woods Hole Research Center, Massachusetts, for his technical and scientific review of the manuscript.

This subject was first explored by Laurence Pringle in *Global Warming: Assessing the Greenhouse Threat*, published by Arcade Publishing/Little, Brown and Company in 1991. Though similarly structured, this edition has been thoroughly revised, updated, and reformatted, and contains new factual material and photographs.

Permission to use the following photographs is gratefully acknowledged:

AP/Wide World, 26, 29, 32; National Aeronautics and Space Administration, 4; National Park Service, 8 (John Kauffmann); Photo Researchers, 20 (Nigel Cattlin, Holt Studios International), 24 (Philippe Bourseiller), 39 (Grantpix); Laurence Pringle, 10, 13, 19, 21, 31, 33, 44; Visuals Unlimited, 5, 6 (William Weber), 7 (David Cavagnaro), 12 (Hal Beral), 14 (G. Prance), 15 (Mark E.), 17 (Steve McCutcheon), 18 (Betty Sederquist), 22 (Frank Hanna), 25 (Perron), 27 (Mark A. Schneider), 30 (Tom J. Ulrich), 35 (Bill Kamin), 37 (Inga Spence), 41, 43 (Steve McCutcheon); Scott Willis, San Jose Mercury News, 42.

Diagrams: 9, 16, based on data from the National Oceanic and Atmospheric Administration; 11, based on data from the Environmental Protection Agency; 38, based on data from the Intergovernmental Panel on Climate Change. Diagrams on 9 and 11 by Ann Neumann.

Text © 2001 by Laurence Pringle

First published in the United States in 2001 by SeaStar Books, a division of North-South Books Inc., New York. Published simultaneously in Great Britain, Canada, Australia, and New Zealand by North-South Books, an imprint of Nord-Süd Verlag AG, Gossau Zürich, Switzerland. First SeaStar Books paperback edition published in 2003.

Library of Congress Cataloging-in-Publication Data
Pringle, Laurence P.
Global warming: the threat of Earth's changing climate / Laurence Pringle.
    p. cm.
Includes bibliographical references and index.
1. Global warming–juvenile literature [1. Global warming.] I. Title.
QC981.8.G56 P75 2001
363.738'74—dc21   00-063740

A CIP catalogue record for this book is available from The British Library.

ISBN 1-58717-009-4 (reinforced trade edition)
10 9 8 7 6 5 4 3 2

ISBN 1-58717-228-3 (paperback edition)
10 9 8 7 6 5 4 3 2 1
Printed in Belgium

For more information about our books, and the authors and artists who create them, visit our web site: www.northsouth.com

CONTENTS

GLOBAL WARMING HAS BEGUN

Human activities have changed the chemistry of Earth's atmosphere.

Earth is getting warmer. Summers are growing hotter. Glaciers are melting. Sea levels are rising. The changes are small, so far, but they are expected to grow and speed up. In the twenty-first century, our planet may be hotter than it was in most of the last 420,000 years.

As oceans rise, land and cities along coasts may be flooded. Millions of people may have to abandon their homes, and low-lying islands may disappear completely. Heat and drought may cause forests to die and food crops to fail. Wildlife populations may be wiped out, and countless people may face severe food shortages. Global warming will affect weather everywhere, plants and animals everywhere, people everywhere.

Each year the evidence grows that humans are warming Earth's atmosphere by their everyday activities, including cutting down forests and especially by burning fuels that release heat-holding gases into the air. Some people say that we should wait for more evidence before taking any action, but climate experts from all over the world say that we must act now. Humans can halt global warming, but to do so, people everywhere will need to cooperate more than they ever have before.

This book tells why Earth's climate is warming. It describes the alarming effects of climate change that are already occurring and those that scientists forecast for the years ahead. And it tells what people must do in order to prevent a potential worldwide disaster of their own making.

Over long periods of time, the amount of solar energy reaching Earth has varied.

CLIMATES CHANGE

No tall trees grow in the cold tundra of the Canadian Arctic.

Weather changes from day to day. It may also change from year to year. The area where you live may have an occasional drought or an unusually cold winter. Variations like these are part of overall climate—the weather that prevails in an area over the years.

You can often find slightly different climates in places that are very close to one another. For example, the year-round climate on the north side of a house or even of a tree is cooler than the south side, where more sunlight falls.

Our planet has a great range of climates, from the frigid polar regions to the hot tropics of the equator.

People expect weather to change but often assume that climates are constant. However, climates have changed dramatically throughout Earth's history. Picture the conditions just 18,000 years ago—a short time in the life of a planet that is more than 4 billion years old: The last ice age was at its peak. So much water was frozen in vast ice sheets on land that the sea level was more than 300 feet (100 meters) lower than the current level. The Caribbean islands of today were all part of a single larger island. A broad land bridge existed between North America and Siberia. Glaciers that towered up to two miles high covered much of North America and northern Europe. The last of these ice sheets melted about 7,000 years ago, bringing Earth's oceans near their present levels.

Ice ages are believed to be caused by regular changes in Earth's orbit and its tilt toward the sun. These changes sometimes reduce the amount of solar energy reaching Earth, cooling its climate.

Plants grow lush and a great variety of animal life thrives in a hot, wet climate.

Ice ages are inevitable, and scientists believe another will come, perhaps 10,000 years from now. We cannot avoid a future ice age or other natural variations in climate. In the seventeenth century, there was a cooling and severe winters that climate scientists call the Little Ice Age. Even now, climatologists say, some global warming may come from natural variations in Earth's climate. We can, however, do something about the troublesome climate changes that we are bringing on ourselves.

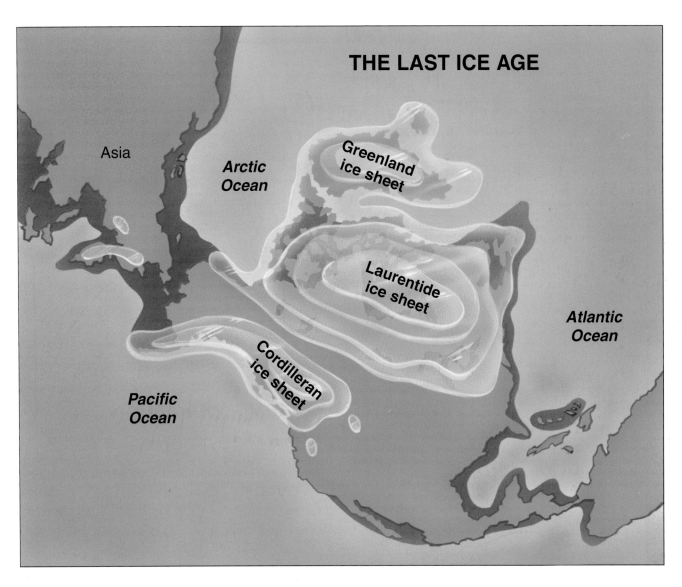

THE LAST ICE AGE

Asia

Arctic Ocean

Greenland ice sheet

Laurentide ice sheet

Atlantic Ocean

Cordilleran ice sheet

Pacific Ocean

Past climate change has affected the amount of water frozen in glaciers (left) as well as the sea level everywhere on Earth. Global temperatures just nine degrees colder than today's caused the last ice age. As the above diagram illustrates, with vast amounts of water locked up in ice sheets, the sea level dropped, exposing the areas shown in brown.

The Greenhouse Effect

The glass or plastic roof of a greenhouse traps heat energy from the sun. Earth's atmosphere does not trap heat in this way. Some of its gases hold heat energy, then release it, warming the atmosphere.

Earth is covered by a thin layer of gases called the atmosphere. Nitrogen and oxygen make up more than 99% of this atmosphere. Nitrogen is about 79% by volume, and oxygen about 20%. Without oxygen, there would be no life on our planet. It enables both plants and animals to burn food for energy. Oxygen also enables people to burn fuels for warmth, cooking, transportation, and manufacturing.

Compared to oxygen and nitrogen, there is only a trace of carbon dioxide in the atmosphere—now about 0.036%. But this gas, along with water vapor, is vital for life on Earth.

When sunlight strikes Earth's surface it is changed to heat or infrared energy. Some of this heat energy is absorbed by soils, plants, and water on the surface. A lot of it is reflected back toward space. Not all of it is lost, however.

Some of this heat is absorbed by molecules of water vapor, carbon dioxide, methane, and other gases. This warms the atmosphere. Because these gases are present in such small quantities, a small change in their concentration can have a big effect on Earth's temperature.

Heat-absorbing gases such as carbon dioxide and water vapor are known as greenhouse gases, and their warming of the atmosphere is called the greenhouse effect. However, Earth's atmosphere does not work like a greenhouse in which plants are raised. In a plant greenhouse, glass or clear plastic traps heat energy. Earth's atmosphere does not trap heat. Water vapor and other greenhouse gases constantly absorb and emit heat energy, so Earth's surface gets heat from both the sun and the atmosphere.

Even though Earth's atmosphere does not actually work like a

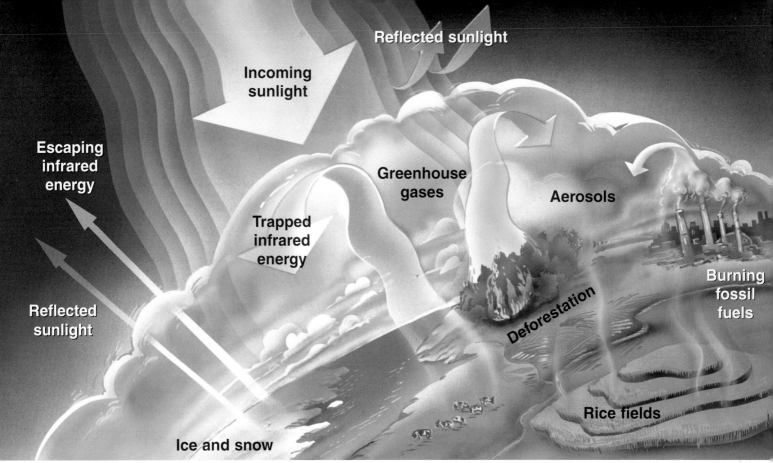

Reflected sunlight

Incoming sunlight

Escaping infrared energy

Greenhouse gases

Aerosols

Trapped infrared energy

Reflected sunlight

Deforestation

Burning fossil fuels

Rice fields

Ice and snow

Some solar energy is reflected into space from clouds as well as from ice and snow. Solar energy that strikes Earth's surface changes to heat (infrared) energy. Some of this energy also escapes Earth's atmosphere. Other infrared energy warms Earth. Human activities release gases that trap more heat in the atmosphere, though tiny air pollutants called aerosols reflect some solar energy and have a cooling effect.

greenhouse, the term "greenhouse effect" has been widely accepted and is used in this book.

Like Earth, the planet Venus also has a greenhouse effect. However, its atmosphere is so rich in carbon dioxide that the surface temperature is about 860 degrees Fahrenheit (441 degrees Celsius). The atmosphere of icy Mars also has abundant carbon dioxide, but the thinness of the atmosphere and the planet's distance from the sun allow for little warming.

Both Mars and Venus are without life. People can be thankful for the small amounts of carbon dioxide, water vapor, and other heat-absorbing gases in Earth's atmosphere. Without these gases, scientists estimate that Earth's surface temperature would be well below freezing. The survival of human life, and all life on Earth, depends on these gases and their warming effect on the atmosphere.

THE CARBON CYCLE

Carbon is stored in coral reefs, ocean water, and sediments in the ocean floor.

Scientists learn about Earth's past atmosphere by studying layers of ancient sediments at the bottoms of lakes and oceans, and especially by analyzing the ice of glaciers in Greenland and Antarctica. By drilling through layer after layer of ice that once fell as snow, they find air bubbles from earlier times. These gas bubbles within glaciers are air samples of the past. From them, we have learned that the amount of carbon dioxide in the atmosphere rose and fell in step with rising and falling temperatures during the past 420,000 years.

Carbon dioxide enters the air during a natural process called the carbon cycle. Carbon is a common element on Earth, present in some kinds of rocks and in coral reefs. Vast amounts of carbon are also stored for a time in soils, in ocean waters, and in sediments at the bottom of the oceans. Scientists are still learning about the carbon cycle, and about where all of the carbon produced each year goes.

When carbon is freed from rocks by erosion, it combines with other elements to form carbon compounds, including carbon dioxide. Green plants take carbon dioxide from the air. Within plants, carbon is converted to compounds that make up leaves, wood, and other plant parts, including seeds, fruits, and leaves that people eat. People, other animals, and plants give off carbon dioxide as they metabolize or "burn" food, and as they decay after death.

Every time you breathe, you release some carbon dioxide into the air. From the air it may be taken up by a plant, the soil, the ocean, or some other part of the carbon cycle. For 420,000 years this natural cycle kept the amount of carbon dioxide in the atmosphere at less than 325 parts per million.

Adding Greenhouse Gases

The amount of carbon dioxide in the atmosphere began to increase in the late eighteenth century because coal was used as the major energy source during the Industrial Revolution. Coal, oil, and natural gas are called fossil fuels because they are made up of carbon compounds from plants that grew millions of years ago. When these fuels are burned, carbon joins with oxygen to form carbon dioxide. Human use of fossil fuels has quickly added large amounts of this gas to the atmosphere.

Burning fossil fuels adds several billion tons of carbon to the atmosphere each year.

Cement-making also adds carbon dioxide to the air, because the process releases carbon atoms from carbonate rocks. In the 1990s, cement-making and fossil-fuel burning combined added more than six billion tons of carbon to the atmosphere every year.

Cutting down forests also adds carbon dioxide to the air. When wood decays, it releases its carbon slowly. When wood burns, most of its carbon escapes quickly in the form of carbon dioxide. Each year, many square miles of forest are burned to clear land for farming, especially in the tropics. This deforestation releases at least a billion tons of carbon each year. Furthermore, it wipes out the trees that would normally remove some carbon dioxide from the air and store carbon in the form of wood and other tissues.

In some developing countries, people desperate for fuel cut down even small trees. Dried cow dung is also used as fuel. Like wood it contains carbon compounds. As a result, carbon dioxide levels in the atmosphere are now about 30% higher than they were in 1860. They reached 340 parts per million in 1987 and 360 parts per million in 1999. These levels are higher than at any other time in human

history. If people continue to burn fuels and destroy forests, the concentration of carbon dioxide in the atmosphere may reach 600 parts per million by the year 2050. This could raise global temperatures higher than they have been in most of the past 420,000 years.

People are also releasing several other heat-holding gases into Earth's atmosphere. These gases add to the greenhouse effect.

Methane gas is released during coal mining and the production of petroleum products. Natural gas *is* methane, so any leaks during the production, distribution, or use of natural gas add methane to the atmosphere. Methane is also produced when forests and grasslands burn, but mainly when once-living materials decay. It arises wherever decay occurs and little oxygen is present—from swamps and rice paddies, from garbage in landfills, and even from the guts of cows and termites.

The concentration of methane in the atmosphere has grown along with the increase in the number of people. Worldwide, cattle are one of the greatest sources of methane. Earth's cattle population has grown with the human population, which totaled more than six billion

in the fall of 1999. There is now one cow or steer for every four people. Each one converts between 3 and 10% of its food into methane.

Methane is not nearly as abundant as carbon dioxide. However, because of the structure of the methane molecule, it is chemically much more effective than carbon dioxide at absorbing heat.

Another heat-holding gas,

The burning of tropical forests to clear land for farming (left) converts stored carbon into carbon dioxide gas. Cattle (above) release methane, which is even more effective than carbon dioxide as a heat-trapping gas.

nitrous oxide, is also added to the atmosphere by the activities of farmers and even by suburban home owners. Nitrous oxide is released when nitrogen-based fertilizers are spread on soils to increase crop yields or the growth of lawn grasses.

Human-made gases called chlorofluorocarbons, or CFCs, also cause the warming of Earth's climate. For decades they were used as coolant gases in refrigerators and air conditioners. High in the atmosphere, CFCs destroy ozone, which shields the surface of Earth from harmful incoming ultraviolet rays.

To protect the ozone layer, steps toward phasing out the use of CFCs were begun in 1987 by international agreement. By 1998, 160 nations had agreed to stop using CFCs. The amount entering the atmosphere has declined and will drop further. (CFCs are part of a chemical group called halocarbons. Other heat-holding halocarbons are also being emitted and need to be reduced.)

Unfortunately, CFC molecules do not break down easily. Furthermore, a CFC molecule is a thousand times more effective than a molecule of carbon dioxide at absorbing heat. For several decades in the twenty-first century, many billions of tons of CFCs will remain in the atmosphere and continue to harm the ozone layer, and also contribute to global warming.

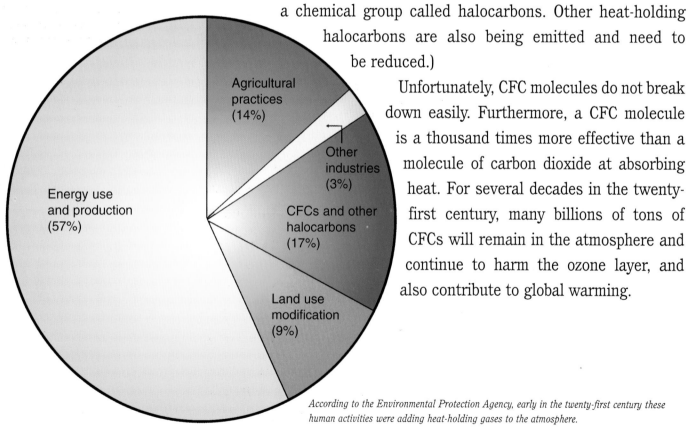

According to the Environmental Protection Agency, early in the twenty-first century these human activities were adding heat-holding gases to the atmosphere.

SIGNS OF A WARMING EARTH

In many parts of the world, temperature records have been kept since 1860. They show that the average global temperature has increased about one degree Fahrenheit over the past century to more than 58 degrees Fahrenheit (33 degrees Celsius). The 1990s were the warmest decade of the twentieth century.

Alaskan buildings, bridges, and highways have been damaged as a warming climate melts permafrost.

Warming did not occur evenly around the world, and some scientists wondered whether the changes in observed temperature might simply be a result of the growth of cities near weather stations. Urban areas form heat islands; pavement and rooftops absorb more heat than soils and plant leaves, so cities have warmer climates than rural areas. Even when this factor was taken into account, however, climatologists still found a worldwide increase in temperature. Ocean temperatures, measured far from cities, also have been on the rise.

Climatologists admit they do not fully understand Earth's climate system. For decades, however, they have agreed that signs of global warming would be most noticeable in cold regions—particularly in the Northern Hemisphere, because it holds less heat-absorbing ocean water than the Southern Hemisphere. They predicted that areas such as Alaska, Canada, and northern Russia would warm more than Earth as a whole. That is exactly what is happening. While the global temperature rose one degree Fahrenheit in the twentieth century, Alaska's temperature rose five degrees in the last 30 years of the century. Large areas of northern Russia have warmed as much, and a similar warming occurred at the other end of the world, on the Antarctic Peninsula.

Alaskan cruise ships used to stop close to the front of the

Columbia Glacier so passengers could watch icebergs break off and splash into Prince Edward Sound. This is no longer possible: The glacier's front has retreated more than eight miles in 16 years. Longer, warmer summers are causing the retreat of hundreds of glaciers in Alaska and elsewhere. The Aletsch Glacier in Switzerland, Europe's largest glacier, retreated more than a mile and lost more than 300 feet in thickness during the twentieth century. And within a few decades, there will be no glaciers in Montana's Glacier National Park.

Permafrost, soil which is usually frozen year-round, is thawing and sinking in irregular patches. This causes forests to drown and highway pavement to crack and sink. Some Alaskan roads and bridges have been abandoned. Vast forests of spruce trees have been killed by spruce bark beetles, whose population has exploded as the climate has warmed. Alaskan farmers have a longer growing season but much less rain than usual.

In Europe, a network of 77 research sites established in 1959 has allowed observers to record the time of the first spring flowers and the dates when leaves turn color and fall from trees in autumn.

In 1993, German scientists found that spring was beginning six days earlier than in 1959 and that autumn was delayed by about five days. A warming Earth had caused an 11-day lengthening of the growing season.

Biologists have predicted that many organisms would shift their ranges toward the poles or to higher elevations in response to global warming. This is now

Since the photograph to the left was taken in 1979, the front of the Columbia Glacier has retreated more than eight miles. Global warming is also causing trees and other plants to flower earlier in the spring.

happening. The range of a checkerspot butterfly in the western United States has shifted northward more than 100 miles. Its most southern colonies have died out. In the Alps, Austrian scientists found that wildflowers were able to grow higher and higher on mountain slopes. Mountain peaks where once little or no life could survive have now become crowded with plants. If the climate continues to heat up, however, these peaks will become too warm and the plants will become extinct.

Overall, a longer growing season could be a boon to farmers. It could allow wheat cultivation to expand northward in the Northern Hemisphere. But global warming can also change rainfall patterns and bring crop-destroying droughts. There are many unknowns about Earth's climate system.

Corn plants withered and died as a result of a drought in Tanzania. Climate experts say that global warming will change rainfall patterns, causing severe droughts in some regions.

Studying Climate Change

Earth's climate system is made up of more than the atmosphere. Climate is affected by the oceans, ice sheets, land, and all life, including humans. It is a complex system, and no scientist claims to understand all of it. Near the end of the twentieth century, however, scientists all over the world were at work trying to learn more about the climate system and how climates change.

Atmospheric scientists are just beginning to understand the effects of clouds on global climate.

When trying to forecast climate change in the twenty-first century, scientists use mathematical models and some of the world's most powerful computers. The models are sets of equations that express the workings of Earth's climate system. Given that some climate processes are poorly understood or totally unknown, these models have sometimes been called "cloudy crystal balls." Forecasts of Earth's future climate have varied quite a bit because scientists have lacked important information.

Until 1989, for example, most computer models of the atmosphere did not include the effects of clouds, a major part of the climate system. Since then, as more is learned about Earth's climate, computer models have taken more of its complexity—including clouds—into account. They have also included the effects of tiny particles called aerosols that are suspended in the air.

Some aerosols come from nature, from microscopic marine algae, and from volcanic eruptions. Many come from the smokestacks of factories and power plants and from the tailpipes of automobiles. They are air pollutants that corrode metals, poison lakes (as acid rain), and harm plant and animal life. In the early 1990s, researchers learned

Tiny particles called aerosols in polluted air reflect sunlight. This has a cooling effect that reduces global warming slightly.

that aerosols have another effect: They reflect some solar energy away from Earth. Some aerosol particles also aid cloud formation. In both ways, aerosols have a cooling effect on the atmosphere.

For several decades, cooling caused by aerosols matched some of the warming in the Northern Hemisphere. Approximately 90% of industrial activity on Earth occurs in the Northern Hemisphere, so aerosols are concentrated there. Between 1950 and 1970, temperatures dropped a bit in parts of the Northern Hemisphere, including the United States. The air was becoming more polluted during that time. Then new controls on air pollution began to take effect. Aerosol particles were reduced. Less solar radiation was reflected back into space, and aerosols no longer hid some of the effects of greenhouse gases entering the atmosphere. (Aerosol particles caused by pollution usually fall to Earth in a few days; methane molecules remain in the atmosphere for a decade, and carbon dioxide molecules remain there for as long as a century.)

Aerosols are now included in computer models of Earth's climate system, and so are clouds, which cover about half of Earth. Clouds are very complex; climatologists sort them into ten types based on altitude, shape, and how they are formed. Clouds have a cooling effect because they reflect sunlight away from Earth, and cast shade. However, clouds also absorb some heat energy from above and below. Much more needs to be learned about the physics and chemistry of clouds. Most climatologists now believe that the warming effect of clouds is slightly stronger than their cooling effect on overall climate.

As Earth's atmosphere warms, clouds may change. Global warming could affect the types of clouds, their altitude, and their water content. These changes could then, in turn, alter the climate. For example, if global warming brought an increase in low, thick clouds, the clouds would reflect more solar rays than usual away from Earth and have a cooling effect. This is an example of feedback, in which a change affects the process that caused it (see sidebar).

Computer models of Earth's climate now include some feedback factors. They also include deep-ocean processes, because the ocean absorbs both carbon dioxide and heat and because its currents move heat from one part of the planet to another. Although models of the climate system have become more detailed, they still simplify the most important forces that drive the climate system; they can never capture the full complexity of Earth's climate.

Confidence in climate models has grown, however. The "cloudy crystal balls" are getting a bit clearer. A volcanic eruption in 1991 produced an opportunity to test the effectiveness of one climate model. The Philippine volcano Mount Pinatubo blasted out 25 to 30 million tons of sulfur dioxide gas, which became a global aerosol haze high in the atmosphere.

In Earth's complex climate system, there are dozens of feedback factors that might influence climate change. Some may speed up global warming. Some may slow it. Here are a few of them:

• *Because snow and ice are white, most of the sunlight falling on them is reflected back toward space. Earth's warming climate is reducing the amount of snow and ice, and more sunlight is falling on soils and plants, which absorb heat energy. This will further warm Earth, causing more snow and ice to melt and even more warming.*

• *A warmer climate will speed the decay of dead plant material, releasing more carbon dioxide and methane into the atmosphere. This will heat Earth's surface more, further increasing the rate of decay and adding even more greenhouse gases to the atmosphere.*

• *An increase in carbon dioxide stimulates the growth of some plants, though the growth spurt may be temporary if soils are lacking in nutrients. Extra growth causes plants to absorb and store more carbon dioxide than usual. This can reduce the heat-absorbing carbon dioxide in the atmosphere.*

This eruption of Mount Pinatubo in the Philippines produced a worldwide haze of aerosols, and a small, temporary global cooling.

This was by far the most massive sun-blocking volcanic eruption of the twentieth century. A climate model at the Goddard Institute for Space Studies predicted that the Mount Pinatubo eruption would cause a global cooling of about one degree Fahrenheit (half a degree Celsius) at its lowest point and would last about two years. That is what actually happened.

THE THREAT OF RISING SEAS

Even without computer models, climate experts agree about many of the changes and problems that rising temperatures can bring. For example, they know that as water warms, it expands and takes up more space. Therefore, whether the atmosphere warms just two degrees Fahrenheit (one degree Celsius) or much more, as some predict, sea levels will rise. Worldwide, tidal gauges recorded an average rise of 7 inches (18 centimeters) during the twentieth century. In the twenty-first century, warming ocean water, along with melt-waters from glaciers and ice sheets, is predicted to rise at least another 20 inches (50 centimeters).

A rising sea level threatens coastal communities, especially when hurricanes strike.

Polar ice sheets are already melting. Since 1993, the southern Greenland ice sheet has lost about two cubic miles of ice annually. In Antarctica, scientists are looking for signs of change in the vast West Antarctic ice sheet. About 120,000 years ago, scientists believe, it collapsed into the ocean and caused a global sea-level rise of 16 feet (4.8 meters). Today that would flood cities all over the world and displace an estimated 37% of Earth's people who live within 60 miles (100 kilometers) of a coastline. Scientists believe that there is no immediate threat of such a disaster, but a century or two of unchecked warming could cause this catastrophe.

Even moderate rises in sea level do great harm, more than the obvious beach erosion and destruction of oceanfront vacation homes. They wipe out the coastal marshes that are vital nurseries for fish and other ocean life. Underground, rising sea levels carry salt water inland and pollute freshwater wells used by millions of people for drinking water.

A rising sea level threatens human survival on island nations and other low-lying land areas. An organization called the Alliance of Small Island States advocates a strong international effort to reduce greenhouse-gas emissions. Its members include the Bahamas, Cuba, Cyprus, Haiti, Jamaica, the Marshall Islands, and the Maldives. They fear being flooded out of existence.

River deltas are also vulnerable to rising seas. Vast amounts of agricultural land could be lost at the deltas of the Indus River in Pakistan, the Chang in China, the Nile in Egypt, and the Mississippi in the United States. Bangladesh sits atop one of the world's largest deltas, deposited by the Ganges and other rivers. One of the most densely populated nations on Earth, Bangladesh suffers from annual floods and storm surges of cyclones, or hurricanes. Rising seas would allow storm-driven water to surge far inland and could submerge more than 10% of the country. In Bangladesh alone, millions of people might become refugees, made homeless by global warming.

Bangladesh is one of several nations that are especially vulnerable to rising sea levels. Flooding in 1998 forced more than 20 million people from their homes.

CHANGING WEATHER PATTERNS

Whether Earth's climate is warmed by some natural sun cycle or by greenhouse gases produced by humans, climate scientists can predict some changes in the weather. A warmer world is a wetter world. Increased heat causes more water to evaporate into the air. This produces more rain and snow worldwide, but weather patterns are likely to shift, bringing droughts to some regions and increased rain to others.

A warming climate causes an increase in tornadoes, hurricanes, and other violent storms.

A warmer world is a world of weather extremes. Instead of the gentle rains preferred by farmers, there will be more heavy storms that cause flooding and erosion. There will be more violent thunderstorms, tornadoes, and hurricanes. These may be called natural disasters, but evidence is growing that humans are influencing them by adding greenhouse gases to the atmosphere. The 1990s saw disastrous floods, storms, and other calamities, including vast fires in Indonesian tropical forests that are normally too moist to burn but that were dried by drought.

Some climatologists believe that global warming is influencing a weather pattern known as El Niño. This pattern acts as a sort of relief valve for excess heat that builds up in the tropical west Pacific Ocean. About every four to seven years, a vast store of warm water pushes east until it reaches the coast of South America. This shift alters ocean currents, changes wind patterns, and triggers both powerful storms and droughts all over the world.

The El Niño of 1997–98 was especially strong and long-lasting. It followed another powerful El Niño in 1982–83. This is unusual, according to researchers who study historical records for clues about past weather patterns. Until recently, strong El Niños were spaced about 42 years apart. Some scientists believe that global warming will quickly recharge heat in the western Pacific. This will bring El Niños that are both more frequent and more intense.

As powerful as El Niño can be, it is just one of many weather patterns in Earth's climate system. Among climate scientists, there is growing concern that global warming may disrupt other patterns and cause dramatic changes. One of the world's most respected climate scientists, Dr. Wallace Broecker of the Lamont-Doherty Earth Observatory in New York, is especially concerned about a change in a huge ocean current called the "conveyor belt." Equal to the flow of 100 Amazon Rivers, it carries warm waters from the North Pacific across the Indian Ocean, around the tip of Africa, and up to the North Atlantic. This ocean current helps warm northern Europe and western Asia. Off Labrador and north of Iceland, the direction of the flow reverses. Cold dense water flows southward, all the way back to the northern Pacific.

Studies of deep-ocean sediments reveal that the conveyor-belt current has abruptly shut down in the past, causing a severe chilling of the Northern Hemisphere and global shifts in rainfall patterns. Each time, the current halted because melting glaciers added great volumes of freshwater to the North Atlantic. Dr. Broecker believes that the global warming now underway could have the same effect. Freshwater from both melting glaciers and increased precipitation could stop the conveyor-belt current. This would bring temporary relief from global warming in parts of the Northern Hemisphere but also cause severe droughts and other climate disruptions worldwide.

Scientists long believed that Earth's climate system changed slowly. Now they know that it sometimes produces drastic shifts in temperatures in periods as short as five years. Referring to the greenhouse gases that people are adding to the atmosphere, Dr. Broecker warned, "The climate system is an angry beast and we are poking it with sticks."

In the late twentieth century and early in the new century, ice storms, droughts, floods, and other weather disasters increased as the atmosphere warmed.

WINNERS OR LOSERS?

Polar bears spend most of their lives on the ice of the Arctic Ocean, which has thinned dramatically in the last few decades.

The global warming that has occurred so far has had both good and bad effects. Milder winters have cut costs of heating and snow clearing in parts of the Northern Hemisphere. On the other hand, hotter summers have increased air-conditioning costs. Unusual heat waves have killed great numbers of people. More than 500 died in Chicago in 1995, when record-breaking nighttime heat and humidity allowed no relief from daytime heat stress.

Agriculture in Canada, northern Europe, and other northern regions may benefit from longer growing seasons and increased rainfall. Heat and drought farther south may cut crop yields. The interiors of large continents are expected to warm up and dry out. Global warming could harm or even halt grape production for wine in California's Napa Valley and in the wine-producing regions of France—areas that were specifically chosen because of their favorable climate. Wine makers may need to seek land to the north to establish new vineyards.

As past ice ages came and went, plants and animals usually had thousands of years to adapt to changing conditions. When the climate warmed, forests and wildlife species gradually moved northward. (Plants do not really move, of course, but extend their ranges as their seeds disperse.) This process requires centuries, not a few decades. Rapid global warming may destroy forests and wildlife over large areas.

Many species may become extinct as their habitats disappear. Polar bears, for example, get most of their food by hunting for seals on ice floes of the Arctic Ocean. They could die out if the Arctic Ocean were to become completely ice-free in the summer. This is a real possibility: Floating ice of the Arctic Ocean lost 40% of its depth in the last four decades of the twentieth century.

Warming seas also affect other life. The 1997–98 El Niño pushed unusually warm water northward along the western coast of North America. Seals and seabirds died when the fish that are their usual prey also moved northward or to deeper waters. A Canadian fisheries expert has found that salmon are adapted to a narrow range of cold temperatures while in the ocean. He predicts that global warming in the next half-century will cause salmon to disappear from much of the North Pacific.

Most of North America's monarch butterflies migrate to winter refuges in cool forests on mountaintops of central Mexico. Rising temperatures may gradually wipe out these special habitats—and the monarchs whose survival depends on them. There is no way to protect national parks or other nature reserves from global warming. According to research by a Dutch scientist, major changes in plant life will occur in a quarter of the world's parks and other protected natural areas by 2050.

Monarch butterflies are just one of many species whose survival may be threatened by changes in habitat caused by global warming.

Some species will thrive in a warming climate. Unfortunately they include disease-carrying mosquitoes, parasites, and pests of crops and livestock. Some medical experts warn that global warming will bring a worldwide spread of infections. They believe that the 1997–98 El Niño demonstrated some of the health risks that may result from global warming. Torrential rains and floods were followed by outbreaks of diseases, especially malaria, Rift Valley fever, yellow fever, and dengue fever—all of which are transmitted by mosquitoes.

However, few of the deaths or infections occurred in wealthy countries. Diseases struck developing nations that lack effective public health programs. In 1997, for example, Texas had a few cases of dengue fever, while nearby areas of Mexico had thousands. Specialists in infectious diseases say that the unstable climate produced by global warming does not have to lead to epidemics if developing countries are given help with defense against the diseases.

Since computer models are not able to accurately forecast the effects of global warming on specific regions, no nation can count on benefiting from climate change. The worldwide prospect includes food and water shortages, millions of refugees from flooded coastal areas, and increased tension between rich and poor nations over scarce resources. It seems likely that every person will suffer in one way or another.

These flood victims hope for rescue in Mozambique. Developing nations are especially harmed by floods, droughts, and disease epidemics caused by global warming.

Obstacles to Change

In 1896, the Nobel Prize–winning Swedish chemist Svante Arrhenius predicted that adding more and more carbon dioxide to the atmosphere would cause global warming. Almost one hundred years later, the Intergovernmental Panel on Climate Change (IPCC) agreed. The IPCC is made up of 2,500 top climate scientists from 60 nations. They are all investigating various aspects of climate change and trying to understand what is known—and unknown—about Earth's climate system.

Everyday activities in industrialized nations produce most of the world's carbon dioxide and other greenhouse gases.

Scientists of the IPCC have warned that carbon dioxide levels will probably reach 600 parts per million by 2050 and that this may raise Earth's temperature by about 2 to as many as 6 degrees Fahrenheit (1 to 3.5 degrees Celsius) by 2100. In 1995, the IPCC declared that "the balance of evidence suggests a discernible human influence on global climate."

In 1999, the American Geophysical Union, a prestigious group of earth and space scientists, stated that there was a "compelling basis for legitimate public concern" about human-induced climate change. It also stated that remaining scientific uncertainty was no excuse for inaction. Climatologists from all over the world agreed that steps must be taken to reduce greenhouse gases.

There are many ideas for achieving this reduction but they all call for less use of fossil fuels, the main source of carbon dioxide produced by humans. People use fossil fuels for countless activities, including transportation, manufacturing, producing food, and heating, cooling, and lighting homes and businesses. Wasteful use of coal, petroleum,

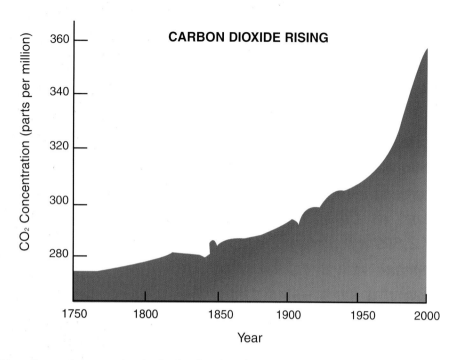

CARBON DIOXIDE RISING

This graph traces the concentration of carbon dioxide in the atmosphere from pre-Industrial Revolution times to the present.

and natural gas can be cut, and alternate sources of energy can be used. The world can be weaned from its dependence on fossil fuels, and some nations and companies have taken steps to do so.

This challenging but vital change faces one main obstacle: opposition from industries and countries that are most threatened by the change. These include the coal and oil industries, oil-exporting nations, the automobile industry, and many manufacturers.

Resisting change, these powerful forces have devoted great effort to deny that there is a global warming problem. They have spent millions of dollars in an attempt to convince the public and political leaders that global warming is a myth, supported by shaky science. Industry groups promote the views of "greenhouse skeptics"—a handful of scientists recruited to criticize the growing evidence that humans are altering Earth's climate and to advance the false notion that climate scientists are divided about that evidence.

Chemicals in solar cells change sun rays directly into electric current. The cost of solar electricity has declined and is expected to fall further, making it competitive with electricity produced by burning fossil fuels.

The overall effort has influenced news media, politicians, and the general public. It has weakened international efforts to take big steps toward reducing greenhouse gases. Nevertheless, the truth about global warming and its effects is beginning to erode obstacles to change. At first the oil industry was united in its efforts. Most major oil companies gave financial support to the Global Climate Coalition, an industry lobbying group. Beginning in the mid-1990s, however, oil companies began to withdraw from this group. In 1995, a spokesman for Shell Oil said, "We have to start to prepare for the orderly transition to new, renewable forms of energy." British Petroleum also withdrew and began to expand work in the solar-energy field.

The unstable climate and powerful storms caused by global warming have already hurt one type of business: the insurance industry. During the 1980s, insurers paid about $17 billion for weather-related losses worldwide. Then in just five years—1990 to 1995—it paid $57 billion for losses from tornadoes, hurricanes, floods, and other weather disasters. The insurance industry relies on the best information available to judge risks and set the terms of its policies. In contrast to the businesses still opposed to action, the insurance industry strongly advocates reducing greenhouse emissions.

REFORESTING THE EARTH

In the past ten thousand years, a third of Earth's forests have been cut down and not replaced. The pace of deforestation has quickened, and it accounts for roughly one-fifth of humans' annual emissions of carbon dioxide.

Destruction of forests, especially by burning, is a major source of increased carbon dioxide in the atmosphere.

Scientists urge that forest clearing be slowed, and advocate a major reforestation effort. All plants take in carbon dioxide and store some carbon, but trees, because of their size and long lives, play an important role in the carbon cycle. (Although, in northern forests, more of the carbon is stored in the soil and debris on the forest floor than in the trees.)

Besides storing carbon, trees have a cooling effect in the summer. This reduces the need for air conditioning, and, in turn, the need for electricity usually generated by burning fossil fuels. Tree planting is one action being taken by more than 300 cities that have joined a Cities for Climate Protection program that aims to reduce emission of greenhouse gases.

Reforestation is an important goal, but huge tree plantations of one species—called a monoculture—absorb less carbon than forests with a natural mix of species. They are also poor habitats for wildlife. Furthermore, protecting trees and replanting forests can give vital help in removing carbon dioxide from the atmosphere, but these actions are no substitute for actually reducing emissions of this greenhouse gas. Remember, most of the excess carbon in the atmosphere was safely stored underground within coal and oil until these fossil fuels were extracted and burned. Trees alone cannot put all that carbon in storage again.

Reducing Greenhouse Gases

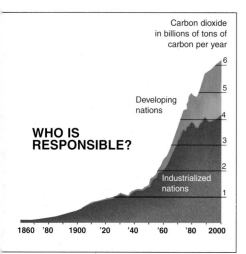

Carbon dioxide in billions of tons of carbon per year

WHO IS RESPONSIBLE?

Developing nations

Industrialized nations

Emissions from developing nations are increasing, but industrialized nations are still responsible for most of the carbon dioxide added to the atmosphere.

People living in cold climates may welcome a little warming, but action must be taken soon in order to limit warming to "a little." Because carbon dioxide lasts so long in the atmosphere, a reduction in emissions now won't have any effect for a century. Also, heat in oceans diffuses slowly to the depths, and oceans give up their heat very slowly. Even if greenhouse gases were reduced sharply now, sea levels will continue to rise for at least two centuries.

These are strong arguments for swift action, but very little has happened. In 1992, more than 150 nations agreed to reduce their carbon dioxide emissions to 1990 levels by the year 2000. These voluntary commitments failed. The next meeting took place in 1997 in Kyoto, Japan. Representatives of more than 160 nations agreed on the Kyoto Protocol—a plan that would require 38 industrialized nations to reduce their emissions of carbon dioxide and five other heat-absorbing gases to 5.2% below 1990 levels by 2012. This is a difficult goal for most countries to achieve but only a first step toward bringing a halt to global warming. To accomplish that, emissions of greenhouse gases must be reduced even further.

The Kyoto Protocol assigned different targets to different countries. The United States was required to cut emissions 7% below 1990 levels. It emits a quarter of all carbon dioxide emissions from fossil fuels. Each person in the United States is responsible for carbon dioxide emissions that are double those of a person in Japan, triple those of a person in France, and ten times those of a person in Brazil.

Automobile makers in the United States are allowed to build gas guzzlers, such as sport utility vehicles, which burn gasoline ineffi-

Auto experts say that gasoline-powered cars are on the way out. Electric cars are now available, as are "hybrid" cars powered by gasoline and an electric motor. Next? Cars with fuel cells that run on hydrogen.

ciently. Government enforcement of a much higher miles-per-gallon standard for cars would cut emissions of carbon dioxide sharply. Fuel used to heat or cool buildings could also be cut by adding insulation and replacing windows. Using energy-saving appliances, lightbulbs, machines, and processes can bring further cuts. These steps in energy conservation are relatively easy. They "pick the low-hanging fruit first," as some economists say. There are many opportunities to reduce greenhouse gases produced by Earth's most energy-wasteful nation, the United States.

If Earth's industrialized nations are to meet their Kyoto goals, which are to take effect between 2008 and 2012, they must begin to reduce the use of coal or to use modern technology that burns it efficiently. Coal contains more carbon than oil and twice as much as natural gas. Wood and other plant products (including paper separated from household waste) produce less carbon dioxide than coal but more than natural gas.

No carbon dioxide at all comes from energy sources such as nuclear power (though fossil fuels are used in mining and processing uranium, the nuclear fuel). However, many people are concerned about nuclear power's cost and safety, including the disposal of nuclear waste. Clean, safe sources of electricity include water, wind, and solar power. New wind turbines produce electricity at about the same cost as new coal-fired plants. The cost of making electricity from sun energy has also dropped, and many electric utilities are expected to build solar energy plants in the twenty-first century.

Growing numbers of companies see global warming as a great opportunity. They are rapidly developing new products, such as combustion-free fuel cells, and creating manufacturing processes that reduce use of fossil fuels. Automobile makers have begun to admit that the days of gasoline-powered engines are numbered and are developing engines for other fuels, such as hydrogen.

An intriguing new idea is carbon management. Research is underway to see if carbon can be captured when coal or another fossil fuel is burned, with the carbon then being injected deep in the ocean or stored deep underground. However, the idea raises questions about effects on nature, including ocean life and ocean chemistry.

If the goals of the Kyoto Protocol are met by 2012, some business leaders and economists predict a crushing blow to the world economy. Industry groups in the United States spent millions of dollars to persuade the American public that cuts in use of fossil fuels will bring financial disaster. Others disagree. In 1996, two thousand economists, including four Nobel Prize winners, signed a statement that the benefits of action on global warming outweigh the costs. Some energy experts say that a trend toward low carbon fuels is well underway and will eventually lead to what they call the "decarbonization" of human energy systems.

Electricity generated by modern wind turbines is often cheaper than that from coal-fired power plants. Wind power is one of the world's most rapidly growing industries.

Global warming could lead to global disaster. The actions needed to reduce greenhouse gases also make good sense for other reasons. People save money by using fuels more efficiently. They produce less pollution. Halting deforestation reduces erosion, conserves water, and prevents the loss of many unique plants and animals that may someday prove to be invaluable to people.

Moreover, many of the devices and processes that can replace fossil fuels are already available. A basic change in the world's energy diet is possible, but it will be hard and sometimes economically painful to achieve. However, the best information available on Earth's climate system makes it clear that the alternative—business as usual, doing nothing—is no longer a choice.

People everywhere, rich and poor, have a stake in this vital matter. The Kyoto Protocol called for Earth's industrialized nations to take the first step. These nations account for about 30% of Earth's population but produce about 75% of greenhouse gases. It seemed fair to many people that the industrialized nations "go first." In the United States, however, Congress refused to ratify the terms of the Kyoto Protocol unless developing nations were also required to take action.

These less wealthy nations aim to industrialize, as other countries did, by burning fossil fuels. China, home to one-sixth of Earth's population, has great reserves of coal. Relying on this fuel, China may surpass the United States as the biggest source of carbon dioxide by 2025.

Global warming cannot be stopped unless China and other developing nations are persuaded to bypass fossil fuels as the key to industrialization. The Kyoto Protocol offered a program called the Clean Development

China's reliance on coal for energy causes severe air pollution and acid rain, and contributes to global warming.

Mechanism that may help. It is aimed at rewarding companies and industrialized nations that give money and equipment to developing nations to help them reduce their use of fossil fuels.

Many developing nations lie in the tropics, where solar energy is abundant all year. They stand to gain the most from development of low-cost solar power. Wealthy nations can help themselves and everyone on Earth if they help poorer nations develop solar energy and other alternatives to fossil fuels.

The Kyoto Protocol was only a small first step toward solving this complex and difficult problem. Earth's population continues to grow, and with it so do emissions of greenhouse gases. Disturbing signs of climate change also grow more common.

Meeting people's needs for food and energy while reducing greenhouse gases is the greatest challenge ever faced by humans. Solving these problems will require extraordinary cooperation among nations.

Can humankind rise to this challenge?

GLOSSARY

aerosols—tiny bits of liquid or solid matter suspended in air. They come from natural sources such as erupting volcanoes and from waste gases emitted from automobiles, factories, and power plants. By reflecting sunlight, aerosols cool the climate and offset some warming caused by greenhouse gases.

atmosphere—the mass of gases that surround Earth. The atmosphere reaches 400 miles above the surface, but 80% of its air is concentrated in the troposphere, which extends seven miles upward. Although nitrogen and oxygen make up 99% of Earth's atmosphere, other atmospheric gases are vital for the survival of life on Earth.

carbon cycle—the natural movement of carbon through nature, and through both living and nonliving things. For example, carbon atoms are released from the surface of limestone rocks and enter the air as part of carbon dioxide molecules, which are later absorbed by plants. The carbon atoms become parts of leaves or fruits that are eaten by animals. Decay of animals may release carbon into the soil, or into the air again.

carbon dioxide—a colorless, odorless gas that forms when carbon atoms combine with oxygen atoms—for example, during the process of burning or of decay. Carbon dioxide is a tiny but vital part of the atmosphere. It is a key ingredient in photosynthesis, the process by which green plants make the food upon which all animals depend. The heat-absorbing ability of carbon dioxide helps make life on Earth possible.

chlorofluorocarbons (CFCs)—gases once widely used as coolants in refrigerators and air conditioners, as foaming agents for insulation and food packaging, and as cleaning agents in certain industries. CFCs are long-lasting compounds that absorb heat energy more effectively than carbon dioxide. In the upper atmosphere, chlorine from CFCs destroys ozone, which protects life on Earth from harmful ultraviolet radiation. An international treaty calls for all production of CFCs to cease by the year 2010.

climate—the weather conditions that prevail through the years in a specific area. Climates of rather small areas (for example, of one side of a valley or a tree) are called microclimates.

climatologists—scientists who study climates. Others who are involved in learning about global climate change include computer programmers and scientists who study oceans, glaciers, weather, and the atmosphere.

delta—the deposit of mud, silt, and other sediments that have been carried by a river or stream to its mouth. Deltas of major rivers are usually prized as highly fertile farmland.

El Niño—a weather pattern that originates in the tropical western Pacific Ocean. Its full name is El Niño Southern Oscillation. Every few years, the temperature of the western Pacific rises several degrees above that of waters to the east. The warmer water moves eastward, causing shifts in ocean currents, jet-stream winds, and weather in both the Northern and Southern Hemispheres.

evaporation—the process by which a liquid, such as water, is changed to a gas.

feedback—a change caused by a process that, in turn, may influence that process. Some

changes caused by global warming may hasten the process of warming (positive feedback); some may slow warming (negative feedback).

fossil fuels—fuels containing carbon that formed from living materials millions of years ago. Coal, natural gas, and petroleum are fossil fuels.

greenhouse effect—a warming effect that occurs in Earth's atmosphere as carbon dioxide and other gases absorb heat energy and emit heat that reaches Earth's surface. The greenhouse effect makes Earth a habitable planet. On Venus, the greenhouse effect is so great that it creates conditions too hot for life.

Industrial Revolution—the change from making products with hand tools in small workshops to making them with machines in factories. The development of the Watt steam engine in 1763 was a vital key; in 1785 steam engines fueled by coal provided power for the first successful steam textile factory in England. As industries burned more and more coal and other fossil fuels, the amount of carbon dioxide in the atmosphere increased.

infrared—invisible heat radiation that is emitted by the sun and by virtually every warm substance or object—rocks, water, buildings, hot coals, and living things, including humans.

methane—a colorless, odorless, flammable gas that is the major ingredient of natural gas. Methane is produced wherever decay occurs and little or no oxygen is present.

molecule—the smallest amount of a compound that has the characteristics of that substance. A molecule of carbon dioxide consists of two atoms of oxygen and one of carbon.

monoculture—a large area of forest or farmland planted with one species of plant. Whether made of trees, corn, or other plants, monocultures are more vulnerable than more diverse plantings to outbreaks of pests or diseases.

nitrogen—in the form of a gas, nitrogen takes up four-fifths of the volume of Earth's atmosphere. Nitrogen is also an element in substances such as proteins, fertilizers, and ammonia.

nitrous oxide—a heat-absorbing gas in Earth's atmosphere. Nitrous oxide is emitted from nitrogen-based fertilizers.

nuclear power—electricity produced by a process that begins with the splitting apart of uranium atoms, yielding great amounts of heat energy. The word "nuclear" refers to the nucleus or center of an atom.

ozone—a form of oxygen present in small amounts in Earth's atmosphere. A layer of ozone, between 14 and 19 miles above sea level, makes life possible by shielding Earth's surface from most ultraviolet rays. In the lower atmosphere, ozone emitted from auto exhausts and factories is an air pollutant. It damages materials and living tissues and causes headaches and burning eyes.

permafrost—a layer of soil in Arctic regions that is normally frozen year-round. The soil above it thaws in the summer and this allows some plant growth.

tundra—a treeless habitat of the Arctic. Beneath its covering of mosses, lichens, and stunted shrubs lies permafrost—subsoil that is frozen year-round.

ultraviolet—invisible radiation from the sun that has shorter wavelengths than visible violet light. Ultraviolet light includes tanning rays and more dangerous wavelengths that cause sunburn and skin cancer. Most of these damaging rays are blocked from reaching Earth's surface by a layer of ozone in the stratosphere.

weather—conditions of the atmosphere at a particular time and place, including temperature, precipitation, air pressure, and wind speed and direction.

FURTHER READING

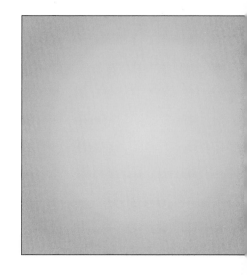

Abramovitz, Janet. "Unnatural Disasters." *World Watch,* July-August, 1999, pp. 31–35.

Christianson, Gale. *Greenhouse: The 200-Year Story of Global Warming.* New York: Walker, 1999.

Culotta, Elizabeth. "Will Plants Profit From High CO_2?" *Science,* May 5, 1995, pp. 654–656.

D'Agnese, Joseph. "Why Has Our Weather Gone Wild?" *Discover,* June 2000, pp. 72–78.

Dwyer, Gary. "Unraveling the Signals of Global Climate Change." *Science,* January 14, 2000, pp. 246–247.

Epstein, Paul. "Climate and Health." *Science,* July 16, 1999, pp. 347–348.

Gelbspan, Ross. *The Heat is On: The High Stakes Battle over Earth's Threatened Climate.* Reading, MA: Addison Wesley, 1997.

Karl, Thomas and Kevin Trenberth. "The Human Impact on Climate." *Scientific American,* December 1999, pp. 100–105.

Kerr, Richard. "Global Warming: Draft Report Affirms Human Influence." *Science,* April 28, 2000, pp. 589–590.

Kiehl, Jeffrey. "Solving the Aerosol Puzzle." *Science,* February 26, 1999, pp. 1273–1275.

Schneider, Stephen. *Laboratory Earth: The Planetary Gamble We Can't Afford to Lose.* New York: Basic Books, 1997.

Simpson, Sarah. "Melting Away." *Scientific American,* January 2000, pp. 19–20.

Stevens, Wallace. "Arctic Thawing May Jolt Sea's Climate Belt." *The New York Times,* December 7, 1999, p. F5.

Stevens, Wallace. "Human Imprint on Climate Change Grows Clearer." *The New York Times,* June 29, 1999, pp. F1, F9.

Stevens, Wallace. "1999 Continues Warming Trend Around Globe." *The New York Times,* December 19, 1999, pp. A1, A16.

Stevens, Wallance. "Seas and Soils Emerge as Keys to Climate." *The New York Times,* May 16, 2000, pp. F1, F4.

Suplee, Curt. "Unlocking the Climate Puzzle." *National Geographic,* May 1998, pp. 38–70.

Vinnilov, Konstantin, et al. "Global Warming and Northern Hemisphere Sea Ice Extent." *Science,* December 3, 1999, pp. 1934–1937.

Wigley, Tom. *The Science of Climate Change: Global and U.S. Perspectives.* Arlington, VA: Pew Center on Global Climate Change, 1999.

Wuethrich, Bernice. "How Climate Change Alters Rhythms of the Wild." *Science,* February 4, 2000, pp. 793–795.

INDEX

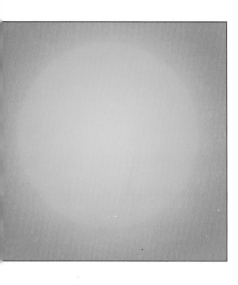